D0250871

 Bellocq's Ophelia

Other Books by Natasha Trethewey

Native Guard
Domestic Work

Bellocq's Ophelia

Poems by

NATASHA TRETHEWEY

Graywolf Press

Copyright © 2002 by Natasha Trethewey

Publication of this volume is made possible in part by a grant provided by the Minnesota State Arts Board, through an appropriation by the Minnesota State Legislature, a grant from the Wells Fargo Foundation Minnesota, and a grant from the National Endowment for the Arts. Significant support has also been provided by the Bush Foundation; the Lannan Foundation; Marshall Field's Project Imagine with support from the Target Foundation; the McKnight Foundation; and other generous contributions from foundations, corporations, and individuals. To these organizations and individuals we offer our heartfelt thanks.

Published by Graywolf Press
250 Third Avenue North, Suite 600
Minneapolis, Minnesota 55401
All rights reserved.

www.graywolfpress.org

Published in the United States of America

ISBN: 978-1-55597-359-9

8   10   12   13   11   9   7

Library of Congress Control Number: 2001096552

Cover Photograph: E. J. Bellocq, *Storyville Portrait,* ca. 1912. © Lee Friedlander, courtesy Fraenkel Gallery, San Francisco.

Cover Design: Scott Sorenson

Acknowledgments

Thanks to the editors of the following journals in which these poems, sometimes in different versions, first appeared:

Callaloo: "Letter Home," "Vignette"
Kestrel: "Letters from Storyville"
New England Review: "Countess P—'s Advice for New Girls"
Shenandoah: "Storyville Diary"
Southern Humanities Review: "Letter from Storyville, December 1910"
The Southern Review: "Bellocq's Ophelia"

"Bellocq's Ophelia" also appeared in *Giant Steps: The New Generation of African American Writers*, edited by Kevin Young, published by Harper Perennial, 2000.

"Photograph of a Bawd Drinking Raleigh Rye" appeared in *The New Young American Poets: An Anthology*, edited by Kevin Prufer, published by Southern Illinois University Press, 2000.

"Letter from Storyville, December 1910" also appeared in *Buck and Wing: Southern Poetry at the Millennium*, a special issue of *Shenandoah*, edited by R. T. Smith, 2000.

"Storyville Diary" first appeared in *The Grolier Poetry Prize Annual 1999*.

My gratitude as well to the National Endowment for the Arts, the Bunting Fellowship Program of the Radcliffe Institute for Advanced Study at Harvard University, Auburn University, the Alabama State Council on the Arts, and the Barbara Deming Memorial Fund for their generous support of this work.

for Brett

Contents

III

. . . she had nothing to fall back on; not maleness, not whiteness, not ladyhood, not anything. And out of the profound desolation of her reality she may well have invented herself.

— TONI MORRISON

Nevertheless, the camera's rendering of reality must always hide more than it discloses.

— SUSAN SONTAG

Bellocq's Ophelia

—from a photograph, circa 1912

In Millais's painting, Ophelia dies faceup,
eyes and mouth open as if caught in the gasp
of her last word or breath, flowers and reeds
growing out of the pond, floating on the surface
around her. The young woman who posed
lay in a bath for hours, shivering,
catching cold, perhaps imagining fish
tangling in her hair or nibbling a dark mole
raised upon her white skin. Ophelia's final gaze
aims skyward, her palms curling open
as if she's just said, *Take me.*

I think of her when I see Bellocq's photograph—
a woman posed on a wicker divan, her hair
spilling over. Around her, flowers—
on a pillow, on a thick carpet. Even
the ravages of this old photograph
bloom like water lilies across her thigh.
How long did she hold there, this other
Ophelia, nameless inmate in Storyville,
naked, her nipples offered up hard with cold?

The small mound of her belly, the pale hair
of her pubis—these things—her body
there for the taking. But in her face, a dare.
Staring into the camera, she seems to pull
all movement from her slender limbs
and hold it in her heavy-lidded eyes.
Her body limp as dead Ophelia's,
her lips poised to open, to speak.

I

Ophelia is the imagined name of a prostitute
photographed circa 1912 by E. J. Bellocq, later
collected in the book, Storyville Portraits.
A very white-skinned black woman—mulatto,
quadroon, or octoroon—she would have lived in
one of the few "colored" brothels such as Willie
Piazza's Basin Street Mansion or Lula White's
Mahogany Hall, which, according to the Blue
Book, *was known as the "Octoroon Club."*

Letter Home

—*New Orleans, November 1910*

Four weeks have passed since I left, and still
I must write to you of no work. I've worn down
the soles and walked through the tightness
of my new shoes, calling upon the merchants,
their offices bustling. All the while I kept thinking
my plain English and good writing would secure
for me some modest position. Though I dress each day
in my best, hands covered with the lace gloves
you crocheted—no one needs a *girl*. How flat
the word sounds, and heavy. My purse thins.
I spend foolishly to make an appearance of quiet
industry, to mask the desperation that tightens
my throat. I sit watching—

though I pretend not to notice—the dark maids
ambling by with their white charges. Do I deceive
anyone? Were they to see my hands, brown
as your dear face, they'd know I'm not quite
what I pretend to be. I walk these streets
a white woman, or so I think, until I catch the eyes
of some stranger upon me, and I must lower mine,
a *negress* again. There are enough things here
to remind me who I am. Mules lumbering through
the crowded streets send me into reverie, their footfall
the sound of a pointer and chalk hitting the blackboard
at school, only louder. Then there are women, clicking
their tongues in conversation, carrying their loads
on their heads. Their husky voices, the wash pots
and irons of the laundresses call to me. Here,

I thought not to do the work I once did, back-bending
and domestic; my schooling a gift—even those half days
at picking time, listening to Miss J—. How
I'd come to know words, the recitations I practiced
to sound like her, lilting, my sentences curling up
or trailing off at the ends. I read my books until
I nearly broke their spines, and in the cotton field,
I repeated whole sections I'd learned by heart,
spelling each word in my head to make a picture
I could see, as well as a weight I could feel
in my mouth. So now, even as I write this
and think of you at home, *Good-bye*

is the waving map of your palm, is
a stone on my tongue.

II

Countess P—'s Advice for New Girls

—*Storyville, 1910*

Look, this is a high-class house—polished
mahogany, potted ferns, rugs two inches thick.
The mirrored parlor multiplies everything—

one glass of champagne is twenty. You'll see
yourself a hundred times. For our customers
you must learn to be watched. Empty

your thoughts—think, if you do, only
of your swelling purse. Hold still as if
you sit for a painting. Catch light

in the hollow of your throat; let shadow dwell
in your navel and beneath the curve
of your breasts. See yourself through his eyes—

your neck stretched long and slender, your back
arched—the awkward poses he might capture
in stone. Let his gaze animate you, then move

as it flatters you most. Wait to be
asked to speak. Think of yourself as molten glass—
expand and quiver beneath the weight of his breath.

Don't pretend you don't know what I mean.
Become what you must. Let him see whatever
he needs. Train yourself not to look back.

Letters from Storyville

December 1910   survival

Miss Constance Wright
1 Schoolhouse Road
Oakvale, Mississippi

My Dearest Constance,

I am not out-of-doors as you feared,
and though I've had to tuck the blue, wool suit
you gave me, I do now have plenty to eat.
I have no doubt my decision will cause you
much distress, but still I must tell you—
when I had grown too weary to keep up
my inquiries and my rent was coming
due, I had what must be considered
the good fortune to meet Countess P—,
an elegant businesswoman who offered
me a place in her house. I did not accept
then, though I had tea with her—the first
I'd had in days. And later, too hungry
to reason, I spent the last of my purse
on a good meal. It was to her that I went
when I had to leave my hotel, and I am
as yet adjusting to my new life.

This first week I sat—as required—
each evening in the parlor, unnoticed,
the "professor" working the piano
into a frenzy, a single cockroach
scaling the flocked-velvet wallpaper.
The men who've come have called only
on the girls they know—their laughter

trailing off behind them, their gowns
floating past the balustrade. Though
she's said nothing, Countess is indeed
sympathetic. Just the other night
she introduced me to a longtime client
in hopes that he'd take a liking to me.
I was too shy to speak and only pretended
to sip the wine he'd ordered. Of course,
he found me dull and soon excused himself
to find another girl. Part of me was
quite relieved, though I knew I could not
earn a living that way.

               And so, last night
I was auctioned as a newcomer
to the house—as yet untouched, though
Countess knows well the thing from which
I've run. Many of the girls do too,
and some of them even speak of a child
they left behind. The auction was a near
quiet affair—much like the one Whitman
described, the men some wealthy "gentlemen"
from out of town. Countess announced
that I recite poetry, hinting at a more dignified
birth and thus a tragic occasion for my arrival
at her house. She calls me *Violet* now—
a common name here in Storyville—except
that I am the *African Violet* for the promise
of that wild continent hidden beneath
my white skin. At her cue, I walked slowly
across the room, paused in strange postures
until she called out, *Tableau vivant*, and
I could again move—all this to show

the musical undulation of my hips, my grace,
and my patience which was to mean
that it is my nature to please and that I could,
if so desired, pose still as a statue for hours,
a glass or a pair of boots propped upon my back.

      And then, in my borrowed gown
I went upstairs with the highest bidder.
He did not know to call me

          Ophelia

January 1911

I know you are driven
to such harsh words
first, out of your concern
for me, and second,
out of your gentle piousness
which I still fondly recall—
the modest tilt of your head,
even when you scolded me,
your prayer book tucked
neatly between the cushions
of your settee. My dear,

please do not think
I am the wayward girl
you describe. I alone
have made this choice.
Save what I pay for board,
what I earn is mine. Now
my labor is my own.
Already my purse swells.
I have bought my mother
some teeth, paid to have
her new well dug. Perhaps

you are too delicate to know
of my life here. Still,
you remain my dearest friend
and should not worry

that I won't write. I know
your own simple means
prevent you from helping me
as you would like. Help me only
as you already do—with the words
I crave, the mundane details
of your quiet life.

February 1911

The girls here are of a country sort, kindly
and plain for the most part, with simple desires—
not unlike myself or those girls I knew at home.
They like best, as I do, the regular meals, warm
from the cooks in our own kitchen, the clean
indoor toilet and hot-water bath. We like, too,

the perfumed soaps and fine silk gowns we wear
in the evenings. During the day we dress
as we like—silk wrappers at breakfast—though now
many of the girls wear their underclothes
about the house. They tease me, but gently,
for my proper clothes and the quiet way I take my tea,

afternoons in the parlor. It is then that in my gestures
I see your long fingers fanning out in excitement
as you speak—not the coarse digits of my own hands
after a season in the fields. Perhaps, then,
I do put on a bit, trying to raise my station.
Just the other day I was sullen and spoke too quickly

at them, my tone harsh. *You are what you look like,*
I said, thinking it might cause some change
in their manner, that they might see to carry themselves
as ladies do. I bit down hard on my tongue at the sight
of their faces—fair as magnolias, pale as wax—
though all of us bawds in this fancy *colored* house.

February 1911

There are indeed all sorts of men
who visit here: those who want
nothing but to talk or hear the soft tones
of a woman's voice; others prefer
simply to gaze upon me, my face
turned from them as they touch
only themselves. And then there are those,
of course, whose desires I cannot commit
to paper.

You ask me how I can do this—

In those moments I am again
a young girl, just past thirteen, seeing
for the first time, the luxurious curve
beneath my own breasts. So taken
with this view of myself, I sit too long
staring at my reflection in the bathwater,
the tin tub growing cold as I look
through myself to the gray bottom,
to nothing. Only my shivering
and the chattering of my teeth
jar me back, my skin gooseflesh,
the Braille text of my future.

Or I am back at the farm store,
the man leaning over me, pinching
the tiny buds of my new breasts,
sneering, calling me womanish
as I stare at the linés in the floor

until they blur into one smooth path
leading away from that place—

I am then nothing
but the light I see behind my shut eyelids.

March 1911

It troubles me to think that I am suited
for this work—spectacle and fetish—
a pale odalisque. But then I recall
my earliest training—childhood—how
my mother taught me to curtsy and be still
so that I might please a white man, my father.
For him I learned to shape my gestures,
practiced expressions on my pliant face.

Later, I took arsenic—tablets I swallowed
to keep me fair, bleached white as stone.
Whiter still, I am a reversed silhouette
against the black backdrop where I pose, now,
for photographs, a man named Bellocq.
He visits often, buys time only to look
through his lens. It seems I can sit for hours,
suffer the distant eye he trains on me,

lose myself in reverie where I think most
of you: how I was a doll in your hands
as you brushed and plaited my hair, marveling
that the comb—your fingers—could slip through
as if sifting fine white flour. I could lose myself
then, too, my face—each gesture—shifting
to mirror yours as when I'd sit before you, scrubbed
and bright with schooling, my eyebrows raised,

punctuating each new thing you taught. There,
at school, I could escape my other life of work:
laundry, flat irons and damp sheets, the bloom

of steam before my face; or picking time,
hunchbacked in the field   a sea of cotton,
white as oblivion—where I would sink
and disappear. Now I face the camera, wait
for the photograph to show me who I am.

March 1911

I know well the state of dread you describe,
and news of another lynching where you are
dredges the silt of my memory—days when

my mother would snuff the lamps early,
a thin blanket of whisper and hush over us.
We'd hear danger even in the soft rustling

of leaves. And in the fields, we'd bend lower
to our work. Such things come as less and less
a shock. Everywhere there are the dead and dying—

disease taking them slowly, or violence with its quick
and steady hand. In the paper today, tragedy
in New York City—a clothing factory, so many women

dying in a fire. The place they worked, locked up tight,
became a tomb. I live where I work. Will I die here
too? I read that some chose a last moment of flight,

leaping nine stories to their deaths. Others stayed
inside, perhaps to be burned clean
in the fire's embrace, to rise again through the flames.

April 1911

My Dear Constance,

You are as steadfast as your name
suggests, and I am as mute
as my own namesake.
Such a strange life this is.
Only when I think I know
exactly the work I do
am I surprised, yet again. Today,

a man came up to my room,
and as I turned from the basin
where I dampened a towel to wash him,
he shooed me away, his coat and trousers
still fastened. Afraid, I asked him,
What do you want? He answered only
a repeat of my own question, and when I knew
he meant for me to answer— *What
do you want?*—I could not. I felt as I do

in the dream where I have run, again,
into the tobacco barn at the back end
of the plantation. The light I let in startles
the cockroaches, and they fly from the eaves,
their wings beating toward my face.
The man who comes wears a carnival mask,
and I am the grinning *nigger*
on whose tongue he places a shiny coin.
When I try to speak, more coins fall
from my mouth, and I can't cry out
or say what I want.

Once, I could have said
what I wanted. I might have answered, *Only*
those things that anyone would—clean living,
a place with light and plenty green.
That would have been enough. Though now,
when I think of the cotton field, nettles
pricking my fingers, a circle of shade
from my straw hat, my mother up ahead,
her face sunken where she'd lost her teeth,
the 100 lb. sack dragging behind her
like a bride's train—the life I've led
thus far—I want freedom from memory.
I could then be somebody else, born again,
free in the white space of forgetting.

July 1911

The environment of this place
is such as I never expected—

as if the very flourish
that is nature must rival

what men have made here:
the stone façades of buildings

in Jackson Square, Cabildo
and Cathedral, spires pricking

a tumble of clouds, releasing,
it seems, our daily dose of rain.

And then there are the quaint
rows of houses, whitewashed,

set amongst gardens of trees
weighted with lemons, oranges,

tangled beards of Spanish moss—
verdant, close-clipped yards

choked with all sorts of vines, wild
bougainvillea and its bright blooms.

Wet city, city below sea level. Here
the rain feeds the creeping mold, dulls

the scent of garbage in the alleys, washes
clean the surface of everything, leaves

a temporary shine—the whole city cloaked
in brilliantine, a fleeting, gilded dream.

race

August 1911

It is true, as you imagined, we do
much business here, mainly because
we are known as *octoroons*—
even the darkest among us—
and customers fill our parlors
to see the spectacle: black women
with white skin, exotic curiosities.

We are no surprise to the locals, though
visitors from the North make a great fuss,
and many debates occur between them
as to whether one can tell, just by looking,
our *secret*. The vilest among them say,
I can always smell a nigger.
Others look for evidence—telltale
half-moons in our fingernails,
a bluish tint beneath the skin.

        In the parlor today,
a man resolved to find the hint
that would betray me, make me worth
the fee. He wore a monocle, moved in
close, his breath hot on my face.
I looked away from my reflection—
small and distorted—in his lens.

September 1911

This past week I splurged, spent a little
of my savings on a Kodak, and at once

I became both model and apprentice—
posing first, then going with Bellocq

to his other work—photographing
the shipyard with its myriad lines,

angles I've just begun to notice. I see,
too, the way the camera can dissect

the body, render it reflecting light
or gathering darkness—surfaces

gray as stone or steel, lifeless, flat.
Still, it can also make flesh glow

as if the soul's been caught
shimmering just beneath the skin.

I find myself drawn to what shines—
iridescent scales of fish on ice

at the market, gold letters on the window
of the apothecary shop, sunlight held

in old bottles and jars lining the sill.
In them, the glittering hope of alchemy—

like the camera's way of capturing
the sparkle of plain dust floating on air.

October 1911

Just the other day I fancied myself
a club woman, like you,
in my proper street clothes—

a new bow on my white straw hat,
my white linen jacket cleaned
and pressed, a modest bit of gingham

at the collar. So attired, I ventured out,
beyond the confines of *the district,*
to do my share of good deeds, visit

the sanatorium, a sick *sister*, her body
invaded by the invisible specter
of our work. Bellocq met me there,

set his camera to this scene: *a woman*
standing in the middle of the frame,
and off to the right, barely in the picture,

what she might become—the sick one
sleeping, hospital curtain pulled back,
only her face showing, disconnected

from the body she has begun to lose.
To the left, dressing gowns hanging empty
on the door. And beyond that door,

what you cannot see.

                Later, my visit over,
I walked out into bright afternoon, the sun
harsh, scouring everything—my face

the face a man recognized. (And here
I hesitate to tell you—) I was escorted
to the police station, guilty of being

where I was not allowed to be, a woman
notoriously abandoned to lewdness.
There, I posed for another lens, suffered

indecencies I cannot bear to describe.
You will not see those photographs—
paint smeared on my face, my hair

loosed and wild—a doppelgänger
whose face I loathe but must confront.
I know now that if we choose

to keep any part of what is behind us,
we must take all of it, hold each moment
up to the light like a photograph—

this picture I send you of my *good* work,
a modest portrait for my mother,
even my rough image in a police file.

December 1911

I would like one day, if you would
permit me, to take your photograph, fix
an image of you for my table
to accompany what is left in my head.

I find it harder now, with each month
that passes, to conjure the true lines
of your face, and I fear you've begun
to change just as I have. I believe

I've learned the camera well—the danger
of it, the half-truths it can tell, but also
the way it fastens us to our pasts, makes grand
the unadorned moment. This is how

I hope my lens would find you—turning
from the board, your hands dusted
with chalk, light on your face, your brow
shining, and beneath it your eyes

returning my own gaze. Then you'd hear
the tiny sound of my shutter falling—
that little trapdoor catching light, opening
and closing like the valves of the heart.

January 1912

I think often of our unlikely meeting
your first day in our classroom—how
you mistook me for white, and then
blinked your eyes in wonder at me,
a girl past school age who should be
attending a husband or some honest work,
come to learn, still, beside children.

Nor could you hide your surprise
at the poverty of our library—too few
books to go around, and those we did have
worn nearly to the threads. And all
the children wanting each day to carry
one home. You brought your own
to lend us, and a globe for the corner

of the room. I recall how you spun it,
showed us *Africa*, moving your finger
back and forth across an expanse of blue.
And at our pleading you showed us, too,
where you'd come from. In that moment
the world seemed larger and smaller,
all at once, as I imagined Atlanta so close

that you could travel to us. I marveled
at the places you'd been—Massachusetts,
New York—the word *travel*, no place
so distant that I couldn't dream myself
there. Do you remember that I kept
your copy of *American Highways
and Byways* for months, reading it,

looking again and again at the pictures?
Imagine, then, my surprise at finding
that Countess keeps a library here,
in the brothel! It's a lovely room—
stuffed chairs, a Persian rug, morning
light through the window, a fat dictionary
on one side and a globe on the other.

Better still, I found on her tall shelves
a copy of that same book, and standing
before the window looking eastward,
I imagined the line between us, words
we post to bridge what seems to me,
now, an impossible distance. I lost
myself, for a moment, and found

upon waking from my daydream, the book
clutched to my chest, and the globe
set in motion, spinning beneath my hand.

March 1912

— Postcard, en route westward

At last we are near
breaking the season, shedding
our coats, the gray husk

of winter. Each tree
trembles with new leaves, tiny
blossoms, the flashy

dress of spring. I am
aware now of its coming
as I've never been—

the wet grass throbbing
with crickets, insistent, keen
as desire. Now,

I feel what trees must—
budding, green sheaths splitting—skin
that no longer fits.

Photograph of a Bawd Drinking Raleigh Rye

—*E. J. Bellocq, circa 1912*

The glass in her hand is the only thing moving—
too fast for the camera—caught in the blur of motion.

She raises it toasting, perhaps, the viewer you become
taking her in—your eyes starting low, at her feet,

and following those striped stockings like roads,
traveling the length of her calves and thighs. Up then,

to the fringed scarf draping her breasts, the heart
locket, her bare shoulder and the patch of dark hair

beneath her arm, the round innocence of her cheeks
and Gibson-girl hair. Then over to the trinkets on the table

beside her: a clock; tiny feather-backed rocking chairs
poised to move with the slightest wind or breath;

the ebony statuette of a woman, her arms stretched above
her head. Even the bottle of rye is a woman's slender torso

and round hips. On the wall behind her, the image again—
women in paintings, in photographs, and carved in relief

on an oval plane. And there, on the surface of it all, a thumb-
print—perhaps yours? It's easy to see this is all about desire,

how it recurs—each time you look, it's the same moment,
the hands of the clock still locked at high noon.

III

Storyville Diary

Naming

—*En route, October 1910*

I cannot now remember the first word
I learned to write—perhaps it was my name,
Ophelia, in tentative strokes, a banner
slanting across my tablet at school, or inside
the cover of some treasured book. Leaving
my home today, I feel even more the need
for some new words to mark this journey,
like the naming of a child—*Queen, Lovely,*
Hope—marking even the humblest beginnings
in the shanties. My own name was a chant
over the washboard, a song to guide me
into sleep. Once, my mother pushed me toward
a white man in our front room. *Your father,*
she whispered. *He's the one that named you, girl.*

Father

—February 1911

There is but little I recall of him—how
I feared his visits, though he would bring gifts:
apples, candy, a toothbrush and powder.
In exchange I must present fingernails
and ears, open my mouth to show the teeth.
Then I'd recite my lessons, my voice low.
I would stumble over a simple word, say
lay for *lie*, and he would stop me there. How
I wanted him to like me, think me smart,
a delicate colored girl—not the wild
pickaninny roaming the fields, barefoot.
I search now for his face among the men
I pass in the streets, fear the day a man
enters my room both customer and father.

Bellocq

—*April 1911*

There comes a quiet man now to my room—
Papá Bellocq, his camera on his back.
He wants *nothing*, he says, but to take me
as I would arrange myself, fully clothed—
a brooch at my throat, my white hat angled
just so—*or not*, the smooth map of my flesh
awash in afternoon light. In my room
everything's a prop for his composition—
brass spittoon in the corner, the silver
mirror, brush and comb of my toilette.
I try to pose as I think he would like—shy
at first, then bolder. I'm not so foolish
that I don't know this photograph we make
will bear the stamp of his name, not mine

*

image of "beauty"

sexualizes

Blue Book

— pleasing men & losing identity

—*June 1911*

I wear my best gown for the picture—
white silk with seed pearls and ostrich feathers—
my hair in a loose chignon. Behind me,
Bellocq's black scrim just covers the laundry—
tea towels, bleached and frayed, drying on the line.
I look away from his lens to appear
demure, to attract those guests not wanting
the lewd sights of Emma Johnson's circus.
Countess writes my description for the book—
"Violet," a fair-skinned beauty, recites
poetry and soliloquies; nightly
she performs her tableau vivant, becomes
a living statue, an object of art—
and I fade again into someone I'm not.

40

Portrait #1

—*July 1911*

Here, I am to look casual, even
frowsy, though still queen of my boudoir.
A moment caught as if by accident—
pictures crooked on the walls, newspaper
sprawled on the dresser, a bit of pale silk
spilling from a drawer, and my slip pulled
below my white shoulders, décolleté,
black stockings, legs crossed easy as a man's.
All of it contrived except for the way
the flowered walls dominate the backdrop
and close in on me as I pose, my hand
at rest on my knee, a single finger
raised, arching toward the camera—a gesture
before speech, before the first word comes out.

Portrait #2

—August 1911

I pose nude for this photograph, awkward,
one arm folded behind my back, the other
limp at my side. Seated, I raise my chin,
my back so straight I imagine the bones
separating in my spine, my neck lengthening
like evening shadow. When I see this plate
I try to recall what I was thinking—
how not to be exposed, though naked, how
to wear skin like a garment, seamless.
Bellocq thinks I'm right for the camera, keeps
coming to my room. *These plates are fragile,*
he says, showing me how easy it is
to shatter this image of myself, how
a quick scratch carves a scar across my chest.

Photography

— *October 1911*

Bellocq talks to me about light, shows me
how to use shadow, how to fill the frame
with objects—their intricate positions.
I thrill to the magic of it—silver
crystals like constellations of stars
arranging on film. In the negative
the whole world reverses, my black dress turned
white, my skin blackened to pitch. *Inside out,*
I said, thinking of what I've tried to hide.
I follow him now, watch him take pictures.
I look at what he can see through his lens
and what he cannot—silverfish behind
the walls, the yellow tint of a faded bruise—
other things here, what the camera misses.

Disclosure

—*January 1912*

When Bellocq doesn't like a photograph
he scratches across the plate. But I know
other ways to obscure a face—paint it
with rouge and powder, shades lighter than skin,
don a black velvet mask. I've learned to keep
my face behind the camera, my lens aimed
at a dream of my own making. What power
I find in transforming what is real—a room
flushed with light, calculated disarray.
Today I tried to capture a redbird
perched on the tall hedge. As my shutter fell,
he lifted in flight, a vivid blur above
the clutter just beyond the hedge—garbage,
rats licking the insides of broken eggs.

Spectrum

—*February 1912*

No sun, and the city's a dull palette
of gray—weathered ships docked at the quay, rats
dozing in the hull, drizzle slicking dark stones
of the streets. Mornings such as these, I walk
among the weary, their eyes sunken
as if each body, diseased and dying,
would pull itself inside, back to the shining
center. In the cemetery, all the rest,
their resolute bones stacked against the pull
of the Gulf. Here, another world teems—flies
buzzing the meat-stand, cockroaches crisscrossing
the banquette, the curve and flex of larvae
in the cisterns, and mosquitoes skimming
flat water like skaters on a frozen pond.

(Self) Portrait

—March 1912

On the crowded street I want to stop
time, hold it captive in my dark chamber—
a train's sluggish pull out of the station,
passengers waving through open windows,
the dull faces of those left on the platform.
Once, I boarded a train; leaving my home,
I watched the red sky, the low sun glowing—
an ember I could blow into flame—night
falling and my past darkening behind me.
Now I wait for a departure, the whistle's
shrill calling. The first time I tried this shot
I thought of my mother shrinking against
the horizon—so distracted, I looked into
a capped lens, saw only my own clear eye.

Vignette

—from a photograph by E. J. Bellocq, circa 1912

They pose the portrait outside
the brothel—Bellocq's black scrim,
a chair for her to sit on. She wears
white, a rhinestone choker, fur,
her dark crown of hair—an elegant image,
one she might send to her mother.
Perhaps the others crowd in behind
Bellocq, awaiting their turns, tremors
of laughter in their white throats.
Maybe Bellocq chats, just a little,
to put her at ease while he waits
for the right moment, a look on her face
to keep in a gilded frame, the ornate box
he'll put her in. Suppose he tells her
about a circus coming to town—monkeys
and organ music, the high trapeze—but then

she's no longer listening; she's forgotten
he's there. Instead she must be thinking
of her childhood wonder at seeing
the contortionist in a sideshow—how
he could make himself small, fit
into cramped spaces, his lungs
barely expanding with each tiny breath.
She thinks of her own shallow breath—
her back straining the stays of a bustier,
the weight of a body pressing her down.
Picture her face now as she realizes
that it must have been harder every year,
that the contortionist, too, must have ached
each night in his tent. This is how

Bellocq takes her, her brow furrowed
as she looks out to the left, past all of them.
Imagine her a moment later—after
the flash, blinded—stepping out
of the frame, wide-eyed, into her life.

Natasha Trethewey was born in Gulfport, Mississippi. Her first book, *Domestic Work*, won the 1999 Cave Canem Poetry Prize, a 2001 Mississippi Institute of Arts and Letters Book Prize, and the 2001 Lillian Smith Award for Poetry. *Bellocq's Ophelia* received the 2003 Mississippi Institute of Arts and Letters Book Prize, was a finalist for both the Academy of American Poets' James Laughlin Award and Lenore Marshall Poetry Prize, and was named a 2003 Notable Book by the American Library Association. Her most recent collection is *Native Guard*, which won the 2007 Pulitzer Prize in Poetry. Trethewey currently teaches at Emory University in Atlanta, Georgia.

Text set in Centaur, the roman font designed by Bruce Rogers in 1912–14, based on the roman type cut at Venice by Nicolas Jenson in 1469. In 1929 Rogers chose as the companion italic Arrighi italic, drawn by Frederic Warde in 1925. This italic is based on a chancery font designed by the calligrapher Ludovico degli Arrighi in the 1520s.

Text design by Wendy Holdman
Composition by Stanton Publication Services, Inc.
Printed by Versa Press on acid-free 30 percent postconsumer wastepaper